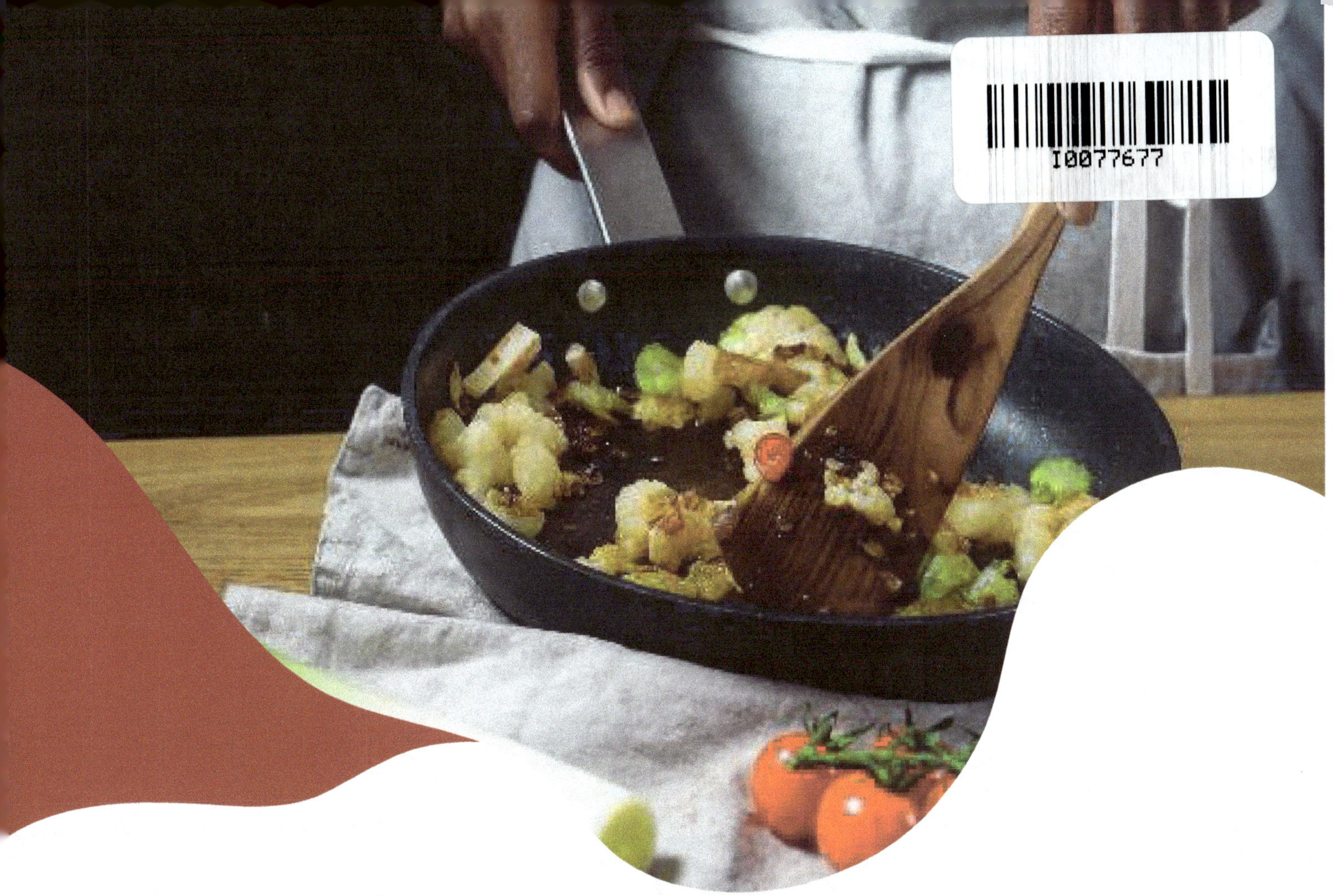

Geez Easy™
COOKING LLC
EASY RECIPES ANYONE CAN COOK

Garcia Stone

DEDICATION

This book is dedicated to every person who has ever stepped into the kitchen with a mix of hope and hesitation. It is for the new cook who worries about getting it wrong, the busy mother who just needs a meal on the table after a long day, and the dad or college student who never imagined they'd be the one responsible for feeding a family. It is for anyone who has looked at a recipe and thought, "This might be too much for me," and then decided to try anyway. My recipes were made with you in mind. They are easy to follow, budget-friendly, and forgiving enough to build confidence one dish at a time.

But more than that, this book is about what food can mean to a family. Cooking isn't only for filling plates, but for filling moments. When we share a meal that is nourishing and flavorful, we lift spirits and bring happiness into the room. When we cook with care, we invest in the health and long life of the people we love most. That is the actual mission of Geez cooking: to give you recipes that serve the body, the spirit, and the soul all at once.

My vision has always been to make healthy, delicious meals accessible to everyone. These recipes encourage fresh herbs and vegetables from the garden when possible, but they also remind you that you don't need much to create something beautiful. Most of the dishes are written for two to four people, because small gatherings can be just as meaningful as big ones.

Each recipe carries a few tips that will guide you beyond one dish, teaching you flavor patterns and cooking techniques you can use again and again. Once you learn the process, you'll see how easy it is to make adjustments, spice it up, or use less if you want, but never lose the flavor that makes the meal complete.

This book is my offering to you, a gift of recipes that are not just about food but about life, love, and connection. May they nourish your family, warm your gatherings, and remind you that cooking, at its heart, is an act of love.

ACKNOWLEDGMENT

Writing this cookbook has been a journey that stretched far beyond the kitchen, and I could never have done it alone. First and foremost, I thank my Lord and Savior, Jesus Christ, God the Father, and the Holy Spirit for saving me, and knowing someone needs help in the kitchen, my deepest gratitude goes to my mother, Anna. Every time I kneaded dough, stirred a pot, or adjusted a recipe, I could hear her voice guiding me with those small but priceless tips only a mother can pass down. She is the true root of everything in these pages.

To my son, Ryan, thank you for believing in me before I believed in myself. Your push to share my first chicken recipe opened the door to something bigger than I ever imagined. To my best friend, Rich, thank you for being my forever taste-tester and never once complaining about eating the same dish five different ways until all were perfected.

I owe a huge thank you to my brothers, Rick, Jamie, and David, as well as my sisters-in-laws, Lisa and Tracy, nephews, Monte, Trayvon, and Jamie Jr, and many cousins. They never let a plate stay full for long and always reminded me that food isn't just for eating it's for gathering, laughing, and creating memories. And to my dear friends, who stood by me during long nights of cooking and endless rounds of recipe testing, your love and encouragement carried me through.

Lastly, to my followers, some of you have been here from the very beginning, trying recipes, leaving comments, and cheering me on. You turned my little kitchen experiments into a shared experience, and for that, I am forever grateful. This book belongs to all of you as much as it does to me.

ABOUT THE AUTHOR

Cooking has always been more than just preparing meals for me. It has been a way to connect, to share stories, and to celebrate life. Growing up in a family where food was love, I learned early on that a good recipe could bring people together in ways words sometimes cannot. My African heritage formed much of my palate, with recipes passed down through generations and memories of kitchens filled with the rich aroma of spices and herbs.

Later in life, my background in chemistry gave me a unique perspective on cooking and nutrition. I began to see recipes not just as instructions, but as little experiments where flavors and textures combined in surprising ways. Travel only deepened that curiosity. From India's spice markets to the cafés of Paris and the kitchens of New England, every journey left me with new inspiration, and those influences you can see in my cooking style.

When the world slowed down during the COVID pandemic, I found myself in the kitchen more than ever before. That pause in time gave me the chance to refine old family recipes and create new ones that were easy, healthy, approachable, and full of flavor. What started as simple meals for loved ones grew into something bigger an aim to show anyone, no matter their skill level, that cooking doesn't have to be intimidating or expensive.

Today, I see myself not just as a cook but as a guide for anyone who has ever doubted their ability to prepare a delicious and healthy meal. Through Geez Easy Cooking, my hope is to give you confidence, joy, and the knowledge that with a little patience and a few good spices, you can create food that nourishes both the body and the soul.

TABLE OF CONTENTS

Dedication	i
Acknowledgment	ii
About the Author	iii
Geez Pesto Spaghetti	1
Geez Teriyaki Turkey Wings	3
Geez Jambalaya Rice Dinner	5
Geez Ultimate Bologna Sandwich	7
Geez Old Fashioned Beef Liver & Onions	9
Geez 1 POT Chicken & Rice	11
Geez Onion Meatloaf	13
Geez Thin Riblets	15
Geez Whitin Fish with Habanero Sauce	17
Geez BBQ Dipped Wings	19
Geez Easy Squash	21
Geez Asparagus & Bacon Potato Cakes	23
Geez African Chicken Stew	25
Geez Indian Tandoori Chicken Stew	27
Geez Whole BBQ Baked Chicken	29
Geez Hawaiian-Flavored Hamburgers	32
Geez Shrimp & Kimchi Noodle Salad	35
Geez Ginger Teriyaki Stove Top Chicken	37
Geez Sweet & Sour Cranberry Chutney Turkey Chops	39
Geez Apple Teriyaki Pork Chops	41

GEEZ PESTO SPAGHETTI

SERVES: 2 – 4

INGREDIENTS:

- 4 Cups of Fresh Basil
- ½ Cup Olive Oil
- 1 1/2c Water
- 2 Stalks of Green Tea Leaves
- 1 Tablespoon Butter or Margarine
- 1/2 Cup Gouda Cheese
- 1/2 Cup Blue Cheese
- 1/2 Cup Feta Cheese
- 1/2 Cup Spaghetti Noodles Per Person

DIRECTIONS:

Step 1: Wash the fresh basil and green tea leaves thoroughly. Place them into a blender or food processor and puree until smooth.

Step 2: In a pan over medium heat, melt the butter or margarine. Once melted, add the pureed basil and green tea leaves mixture.

Step 3: Add Gouda cheese to the pan and stir continuously until it begins to melt and blend with the mixture.

Step 4: For added nutrition, mix in a small amount of Spirulina (optional). Stir well to combine.

Step 5: Allow the cheese mixture to melt completely, stirring for 2–3 minutes until creamy and smooth.

Step 6: Cook spaghetti noodles with water and olive oil, according to package instructions, until al dente. Drain and keep warm.

Step 7: Serve the creamy basil-green tea pesto sauce over the warm spaghetti noodles.

Step 8: Top with crumbled Blue cheese and Feta cheese as desired before serving.

It's Done. Now enjoy your flavorful Geez Pesto Spaghetti!

GEEZ TERIYAKI TURKEY WINGS

SERVES: 2 – 4

INGREDIENTS:

- 2 Fresh Turkey Wings
- 1 1/2 Cups Teriyaki Sauce
- 1/2 Cup Hoisin Sauce
- Poultry Seasoning (To Taste)
- White Pepper (To Taste)
- Granulated Sugar – 1 To 2 Tbsp
- Salt – As Per Taste

DIRECTIONS:

Step 1: Begin by seasoning the turkey wings generously with poultry seasoning. For best results, cover and marinate them overnight in the refrigerator to allow the flavors to penetrate deeply.

Step 2: Prepare your grill and sear the turkey wings on each side until lightly charred. This step adds a smoky flavor and helps lock in the juices.

Step 3: In a mixing bowl, combine the teriyaki sauce and hoisin sauce. Add 1 teaspoon of salt, pepper, and sugar. Stir well to create a rich, flavorful glaze.

Step 4: Brush the sauce mixture generously onto the grilled turkey wings. Once coated, wrap the wings in foil or place them in a covered baking dish.

Step 5: Bake the wrapped turkey wings at 350°F (175°C) for about 40 minutes per 1.5 pounds of meat. This ensures tenderness and full cooking.

Step 6: Remove the wings from the oven, unwrap them, and baste again with the teriyaki-hoisin mixture for an extra layer of flavor.

Step 7: For extra tenderness, steam the turkey wings for 5 minutes after baking. This keeps the meat moist and juicy.

Step 8: Baste the wings one final time before serving. Keep any extra teriyaki-hoisin sauce warm and serve on the side for dipping.

Hot Tip: Sprinkle one teaspoon of granulated sugar over each wing at this stage. This helps caramelize the glaze and enhances sweetness.

GEEZ JAMBALAYA RICE DINNER

SERVES: 2 – 6

INGREDIENTS:

- 2 Cups Fresh or Canned Kidney Beans
- 1 Piece Ham Hock
- 1 Package of Tony's Jambalaya Mix
- 1.5 Lbs of Hamburger

DIRECTIONS:

Step 1: Prepare the fresh kidney beans from scratch following the package instructions. If using canned beans, rinse and drain them before cooking.

Step 2: Place the ham hock in a large pot with water and cook the kidney beans together. This adds a smoky, rich flavor to the beans. Allow them to cook until tender. If using canned beans, cook the ham hock first, then add the beans and let them sit to absorb the flavor.

Step 3: In a separate pot, follow the package instructions for preparing Tony's Jambalaya Mix. Ensure the rice cooks evenly and absorbs all the flavors.

Step 4: While the rice is cooking, brown the 1.5 lbs of hamburger in a skillet over medium heat. Drain any excess fat once the meat is fully cooked.

Step 5: Combine the cooked hamburger and the seasoned kidney beans into the pot with Tony's Jambalaya Mix. Stir well to ensure the flavors blend together.

Step 6: Serve hot as a complete dinner. For extra flavor and variety, add shredded cheese, tortilla chips, and sliced jalapeños on top before serving.

GEEZ ULTIMATE BOLOGNA SANDWICH

SERVES: 1 – 2

INGREDIENTS:

- 2–3 Slices of Beef Bologna
- 1/2–1 Cup White Mushrooms (Or Your Favorite Variety)
- 3–4 Iceberg Lettuce Leaves
- 1–2 Tbsp Miracle Whip or Mayonnaise
- 2 Slices of White Bread

Garcia Stone

DIRECTIONS:

Step 1: Wash mushrooms thoroughly in salt water to remove any dirt and impurities.

Step 2: Slice the mushrooms thinly to ensure even cooking.

Step 3: Heat a small amount of light oil in a frying pan over medium heat.

Step 4: Add the mushrooms to the pan and fry until they are halfway cooked, softening slightly.

Step 5: Add the slices of beef bologna to the same pan and cook until lightly browned and heated through.

Step 6: While the mushrooms and bologna cook, spread Miracle Whip or mayonnaise onto the slices of white bread.

Step 7: Layer the lettuce leaves on one slice of bread for freshness and crunch.

Step 8: Place the fried bologna and mushrooms evenly over the lettuce.

Step 9: Top with the second slice of bread to complete the sandwich.

Slice in half if desired, serve warm, and take a bite of your Geez Ultimate Bologna Sandwich!

GEEZ OLD FASHIONED BEEF LIVER & ONIONS

SERVES: 3 – 4

INGREDIENTS:

- 6 – 8 Pieces of Fresh Beef Liver
- Mildly Greased Cast Iron Grill Pan
- Plain Flour (Enough to Coat Liver Pieces)
- Seasoning Salt (To Taste)
- Tenderizing Seasoning (To Taste)
- Sweet Paprika (Sparingly, To Taste)
- Butter (For Brushing)
- 1–2 Medium Onions (Sliced, For Frying)
- Salt And Black Pepper (To Taste)

DIRECTIONS:

Step 1: Cut the liver into medium-sized pieces. Lightly coat each piece in plain flour and let it rest for 6–8 minutes.

Step 2: Lightly oil a cast-iron grill pan and heat it over low to medium heat. Place the liver pieces in the pan.

Step 3: Sprinkle a small amount of sweet paprika for flavor. Keep the heat low to avoid overcooking.

Step 4: Brown the liver pieces on both sides, turning gently. Add a little salt and black pepper while cooking.

Step 5: Brush each piece with butter toward the end of cooking for added flavor and richness.

Step 6: In the same pan or separately, fry the sliced onions to your desired level of doneness, soft and golden or slightly crispy.

Step 7: Serve the beef liver hot with the onions on top or on the side.

GEEZ 1 POT CHICKEN & RICE

SERVES: 2 – 4

INGREDIENTS:

- 2 large Chicken Breasts
- Badia Chicken Bouillon (or your preferred bouillon)
- 4 cups Jasmine Rice
- 2 cups Warm Water
- Salt, to taste
- White Pepper According to Taste

DIRECTIONS:

Step 1: Place the chicken breasts in a large pot and boil for 5–7 minutes, adding just enough water to cover them.

Step 2: Stir in the bouillon until dissolved for added flavor.

Step 3: While the chicken is boiling, rinse the jasmine rice three times to remove excess starch. This step helps prevent clumping.

Step 4: : Add the rinsed jasmine rice directly into the pot with the chicken breasts.

Step 5: Pour in 1–2 cups of warm water. Aim for a rice-to-water ratio of 1:2 for best results.

Step 6: Cover the pot tightly with a lid and set a timer for 5 minutes. Cook on medium heat.

Step 7: After 5 minutes, turn off the heat immediately. Do not continue cooking past this point.

Step 8: Season the dish with salt and white pepper to taste.

Step 9: Promptly remove the rice from the pot for a firmer, stiffer texture.

Serve warm and enjoy your Geez 1 Pot Chicken & Rice!

GEEZ ONION MEATLOAF

SERVES: 2 – 4

INGREDIENTS:

- 1.5 Lbs Hamburger
- 1 Packet Of Lipton's Onion Soup Mix
- 2 Slices Of White Bread
- 1/2 Cup Milk
- 1/2 Cup Chopped Raw Tomatoes
- 1/2 Cup Raw White Onions

Geez Famous Boss Meatloaf Sauce Topping

- 1 Tsp Mustard
- 1/4 – 1/2 Cup Ketchup
- 1 Tbsp Geez Famous BBQ Sauce
- 1/2 Tsp Onion Powder
- 2–4 Tbsp Ketchup (Optional)

Garcia Stone

DIRECTIONS:

Step 1: Preheat your oven to 350°F (175°C).

Step 2: In a small bowl, soak the bread slices in the milk for about 2 minutes. Mix until the bread breaks down into a lumpy texture.

Step 3: In a large bowl, combine the hamburger meat with the Lipton's Onion Soup Mix. Add the soaked bread and milk mixture, along with the chopped tomatoes and onions. Mix thoroughly until well combined.

Step 4: Shape the mixture into a loaf and place it in a lightly greased baking dish or loaf pan.

Step 5: Bake in the preheated oven for 35–40 minutes, or until the internal temperature reaches 160°F (71°C).

Step 6: While the meatloaf is baking, prepare the topping by mixing mustard, ketchup, BBQ sauce, and onion powder in a small bowl.

Step 7: Remove the meatloaf from the oven, spread the sauce topping evenly across the surface, and optionally add extra ketchup on top. Smooth it over for a glossy finish.

Step 8: Return the meatloaf to the oven and bake for an additional 5 minutes to set the topping.

Hot Tip: Sprinkle 1–2 tsp granulated sugar while making the meatloaf's tomato sauce before baking the meatloaf.

GEEZ THIN RIBLETS

SERVES: 2 – 4

INGREDIENTS:

- 4 - 5 Thin Sliced Beef Riblets With Bone
- 1 - 2 Cups Sweet Baby Ray's BBQ Sauce
- 1 - 2 Red Or Yellow Onions

Geez Famous BBQ Sauce

- 1 Full Bottle Of Sweet Baby Ray's (12 Oz)
- 1/2 Bottle Kinder's Hot BBQ Sauce Or Frank's
- 1/2 – 1/4 Cup Granulated Sugar
- 1/4 Cup Nutritional Yeast (Optional)

- 1/4 Cup Honey (Or 1/2 Cup Grape Jelly If Honey Is Unavailable)
- 1 Tsp Garlic Powder
- 1 Tsp Paprika Powder
- 1 Tsp Ginger Powder
- 1 Tsp Prepared Mustard

DIRECTIONS:

Step 1: Preheat the grill and season the thin riblets lightly with your preferred beef seasonings.

Step 2:: Grill riblets for 3–4 minutes on each side. Be careful not to overcook since they are thin.

Step 3: Brush each riblet generously with BBQ sauce and let them set on the grill for 2–3 minutes.

Step 4: In a grill pan, lightly cook the onions until softened but not fully caramelized.

Step 5: Add the onions to the riblets on top of the BBQ sauce and transfer everything to the oven.

Step 6: Bake for 5 minutes to allow flavors to melt.

Step 7: Let riblets cool slightly, then assemble sandwiches with mayo, lettuce, onions, and tomato on sesame buns or bread of choice.

Step 8: Remove bones before eating if preferred. Serve hot and enjoy!

GEEZ GRILLED WHITIN FISH WITH HABANERO SAUCE

SERVES: 2 – 4

INGREDIENTS:

- 5–6 Oz White Fish (Whitin, Halibut, Or Haddock)
- 2–3 Habanero Peppers (Seeds Removed)
- 1–2 Teaspoons Olive Oil (For Grilling Fish)
- Seafood Seasoning (For Marination)

DIRECTIONS:

Step 1: Rinse the fish fillets under cold water and pat them dry with paper towels. Marinate the white fish (Whiting, Halibut, or Haddock) with seafood seasoning, then refrigerate for at least 4 hours.

Step 2: Remove the seeds from 2–3 habanero peppers to reduce excess heat while still keeping a rich flavor.

Step 3: Heat 1–2 teaspoons of olive oil in a grill pan over medium-high heat. Add the seeded habanero peppers to the pan. Allow them to char slightly, releasing a smoky aroma.

Step 4: Place the marinated fish fillets on the hot pan alongside the peppers. Brown each side, basting occasionally with pan juices, until fully cooked. Cooking times may vary depending on the thickness of the fillets.

Step 5: Refer to a reliable fish cooking temperature chart to ensure the fish reaches the proper internal temperature for safe consumption.

Step 6: Using the grilled habaneros, blend or mash them into a sauce base according to preference. Mix with pan drippings if desired to enhance flavor.

Step 7: Drizzle the habanero sauce over the grilled fish fillets and serve warm. Enjoy!

GEEZ BBQ DIPPED WINGS

SERVES: 4 – 6

INGREDIENTS:

- 1 Full Bottle Of Baby Rays' BBQ Sauce (Approx. 2 Cups)
- 1/2 Bottle Kinders Hot BBQ Sauce
- 1/4 Cup Nonna Pia's Balsamic Glaze
- 1/4–1/2 Cup Granulated Sugar (To Taste)
- 1/4 Cup Nutritional Yeast
- 1/4 Cup Honey (Or Substitute With 1/2 Cup Grape Jelly)
- 1 Tsp Garlic Powder
- 1 Tsp Paprika
- 1 Tsp Ground Ginger
- 1 Tsp Wet Mustard
- Chicken Wings (Use sazon or chicken seasoning)

DIRECTIONS:

Step 1: Preheat your oven and season chicken wings with Sazon or a light chicken seasoning. Bake according to package instructions, but stop 10 minutes before the full cook time is complete.

Step 2: Remove the wings from the oven and let them cool on a wire rack while preparing the BBQ sauce.

Step 3: In a medium saucepan, combine Sweet Baby Ray's BBQ Sauce, Kinder's Hot BBQ Sauce, Nonna Pia's Balsamic Glaze, granulated sugar, nutritional yeast, and honey (or grape jelly).

Step 4: Stir in seasonings (garlic powder, paprika, ginger, wet mustard) for extra flavor. Cook on low heat until the sauce is well blended and smooth. Allow to cool slightly.

Step 5: Dip each wing thoroughly into the cooled Geez BBQ sauce, ensuring they are fully coated.

Step 6: Return the coated wings to the oven and bake for an additional 5 minutes to caramelize the sauce onto the wings.

Step 7: Remove from oven, let cool slightly, and serve warm. Eat these yummy BBQ-dipped wings.

GEEZ EASY SQUASH

SERVES: 3 – 4
INGREDIENTS:

- 3 – 4 Fresh Yellow Squash
- 3 – 4 Pieces of Fatback Meat
- 1 Bunch of Scallions
- 1 Medium-Size White Onion

DIRECTIONS:

Step 1: Cook the fatback in the microwave (3–4 pieces) until it releases oil.

Step 2: In a skillet, fry the scallions and small diced white onion in the rendered fatback oil until almost translucent.

Step 3: Wash and cut the squash into medium-thin slices for better consistency.

Step 4: Steam the sliced squash until slightly tender.

Step 5: Add the steamed squash to the skillet with hot oil and onions. Stir well and simmer over medium heat for 5 minutes.

Step 6: Lower the heat and gently smash the squash in the pot with the onions. Stir lightly to avoid mushing too much.

Step 7: Serve hot and enjoy!

GEEZ ASPARAGUS & BACON POTATO CAKES

SERVES: 2 – 4

INGREDIENTS:

- 4 Large Slices Of Bacon
- 1 Bunch Of Asparagus
- 1 Teaspoon Dash Seasoning
- 1 Tablespoon Brown Mustard
- 1 Teaspoon Truffle Salt
- 1 Teaspoon Crushed Red Pepper
- 4 – 5 Large Potatoes
- 1 Egg
- ½ Cup Bacon Crumbles (From Cooked Bacon)
- Olive Oil For Frying
- Extra Asparagus For Garnish

Geez Holly Sauce

- 3 Egg Yolks
- Juice Of 1 Lime (Or A Squeeze)
- ¼ Cup Ghee
- Teaspoon Brown Mustard

DIRECTIONS:

Step 1: Boil potatoes and mash them.

Step 2: Steam asparagus and mash it into the potato mixture with salt and pepper.

Step 3: Add bacon crumbles to the potato mixture.

Step 4: Lightly fry the potato mixture in olive oil until brown.

Step 5: Make the Geez Holly Sauce by combining egg yolks, ghee, and brown mustard. Add ½ teaspoon of lime juice and mix well. Heat on low for 2–3 minutes, then spoon over the potato patties. Garnish with extra asparagus and enjoy!

GEEZ AFRICAN CHICKEN STEW

SERVES: 6 – 8

INGREDIENTS:

- 8 – 10 Chicken Legs (Cut In Half Horizontally)
- 2 Large White Onions (Cut Into Large Box-Style Pieces)
- 1–2 Habanero Peppers, Sliced (Adjust For Heat Preference)
- 3 Cans Hunt's Tomato Sauce
- 1 Small Can Cento Tomato Paste
- 1 Tbsp Onion Powder
- 1 Tbsp Garlic Powder
- 1 Tbsp Paprika
- 1 Tbsp Dried Basil

- Salt And Black Pepper To Taste
- Light Olive Oil (For Frying)
- 1 Tbsp Sugar (Or More, To Balance Tartness)

DIRECTIONS:

Step 1: Cut chicken legs in half horizontally. Season with onion powder, garlic powder, paprika, salt, and black pepper.

Step 2: Heat a grill pan with light olive oil and cook the chicken pieces until browned and fully cooked on both sides. Remove from the pan and set aside.

Step 3: In a large pot, combine the tomato sauce, tomato paste, dried basil, salt, pepper, and sliced habaneros. Simmer for 5 minutes.

Step 4: Add the chopped onions (large box-style pieces) into the simmering tomato mixture.

Step 5: Transfer the cooked chicken pieces from the grill pan into the pot. Stir gently to coat with sauce.

Step 6: Simmer everything together for 5–10 minutes to allow flavors to blend.

Step 7: Sprinkle one tablespoon of sugar into the sauce (adjust more if needed) to reduce tartness, then taste and adjust seasoning as desired.

Serve hot with rice, flatbread, or your favorite side dish.

GEEZ INDIAN TANDOORI CHICKEN

SERVES: 4 – 6

INGREDIENTS:

- 6 – 10 Pieces Dark Meat Chicken (Legs Preferred)
- 1 (12 Oz) Jar Tandoori Spice
- 1 Tsp Tandoori Spice (Extra For Depth)
- 1 Tsp Ground Turmeric
- 1 Tsp Ground Coriander
- 1 Tsp Ground Cumin
- 1 Tsp Ground Ginger
- 1 Tbsp Ginger Paste

- 1 Tbsp Better Than Bouillon
- 1/2 Tsp Tony's Creole Seasoning
- 1/2 Tsp Sweet Paprika
- 1 Tbsp Butter
- 1 Medium Onion, Finely Chopped
- 1 Tsp Sugar
- 1 – 2 Raw White Potatoes (Cut Into Blocks)
- A Few Carrot Slices
- 1/2 Cup Warm Water
- Baked Potatoes, Noodles, Or Rice
- Raw Green Peppers & Red Onions

DIRECTIONS:

Step 1: Season chicken pieces with the Tandoori spice, extra Tandoori spice, turmeric, coriander, cumin, ginger, Tony's Creole seasoning, paprika, and Better Than Bouillon. Full marination is not required.

Step 2: Grill the chicken pieces on both sides until browned. Then remove the chicken from the grill and place it in the oven, uncovered, at 350°F for 20 minutes.

Step 3: In a separate pan, melt butter and finely chopped onion. Cook until onions are dark and caramelized. Stir in ginger paste and cook briefly until fragrant.

Step 4: Add the Tandoori sauce, chicken bouillon, and sugar. Stir well, then add the potato cubes, carrot slices, and ½ cup of warm water. Simmer for 5 minutes.

Step 5: Remove the chicken from the oven and serve it with the prepared Tandoori sauce over rice, noodles, or baked potatoes.

Step 6: Garnish with raw green peppers and red onions. Serve hot and enjoy.

GEEZ WHOLE BBQ BAKED CHICKEN

SERVES: 2 – 4

INGREDIENTS:

- 1 Whole Chicken (5–7 Lbs)

Geez WC BBQ Sauce

- 1 Cup Jack Daniel's BBQ Sauce
- 1/2 Cup Sweet Baby Rays
- 2 Tbsp Mustard
- 1 Tbsp Soy Sauce
- 1 Tbsp Nonna Pia Balsamic Glaze
- 1–2 Tbsp Kikkomans Soy Sauce

- 2–3 Tsp Texas Pete
- 1 Tbsp Mustard
- 1–2 Tbsp Marcino Cherry Juice
- 2 Or More Red Pepper Flakes
- 1–2 Tbsp Granulated Sugar
- 1 Finely Diced Onion

DIRECTIONS:

Step 1: Rinse the whole chicken thoroughly and pat it dry. Remove the backbone for easier roasting. Marinate the chicken generously with 1–2 tsp Tabitha's Sunshine Spice, 2–3 tsp black pepper, 1 tsp Sazon, 1 tsp onion butter, and 1 tsp sweet paprika.

Step 2: Preheat your oven to 500°F. Place the chicken on a tray and roast for 5–7 minutes. This high heat will give the skin a crisp surface before baking longer. Remove from oven.

Step 3: In a medium pot, combine 1 cup Jack Daniel's BBQ Sauce, ½ cup Sweet Baby Ray's BBQ Sauce, 1 tablespoon mustard, 1–2 tablespoons Kikkoman Soy Sauce, one tablespoon Nonna Pia's Balsamic Glaze, 2–3 teaspoons Texas Pete hot sauce, 1–2 tablespoons maraschino cherry juice, 1–2 tablespoons granulated sugar, a few pinches of red pepper flakes, and one finely diced onion. Cook over medium heat for 5 minutes, then reduce to low and simmer 10–15 minutes, stirring occasionally, and let cool before using.

Step 4: Brush the chicken with a generous coat of the cooled BBQ sauce. Cover with foil and place in a 325°F oven. Bake for 1 hour 15 minutes to 1 hour 45 minutes, or until the internal temperature reaches 160°F.

Step 5: Every 20 minutes, lightly brush on another layer of BBQ sauce for a richer taste. Apply up to 3 coats lightly, depending on how bold you want the flavor.

Step 6: Remove from the oven and let the meat rest briefly, then carve. Serve with extra sauce for dipping.

Hot Tip: Dice and sauté the onion, then add a few pepper seeds to it. Stir the mixture into the sauce while it's cooking.

GEEZ HAWAIIAN-FLAVORED HAMBURGERS

SERVES: 2 – 4

INGREDIENTS:

- 1.5 Lbs Hamburgers
- 1 Tbsp Onion Butter
- Slices Of Fontina Cheese
- Salt & Pepper To Taste
- Zucchini

Geez Hawaiian Sauce

- 1 Bottle Baby Ray's Hawaiian Flavored BBQ Sauce
- 1/4 Cup Shallots

- 1/2 Cup Red Onions
- 1/2 Cup Fresh Strawberries
- 1-2 to Green Jalapeno peppers

DIRECTIONS:

Step 1: Place the hamburger meat in a large bowl. Season it with dry spices, then add ½ cup of Hawaiian BBQ sauce to the mixture. Gently fold the meat so the flavors spread evenly.

Step 2: Divide the meat into equal portions and shape them into burger patties. Press a small dent in the center of each patty with your thumb, this keeps them from puffing up while cooking. Place the patties on a tray and set aside. Save half a cup of the Hawaiian BBQ sauce for dipping later.

Step 3: Lightly oil a grill pan and place it over high heat until hot.

Step 4: Place the patties on the hot grill pan. Cook on high for 2 minutes per side, then reduce the heat to medium-low. Brush onion butter on top and continue cooking until the patties reach a safe internal temperature.

Step 5: Insert three toothpicks vertically into the center of each patty. This helps them cook more evenly, stay compact, and retain their juices.

Step 6: Add onion rings and thick slices of pineapple or zucchini to the pan with the patties. Cook slowly until soft, sweet, and golden brown.

Step 7: In a blender, combine one bottle of Sweet Baby Ray's Hawaiian BBQ Sauce, ¼ cup chopped shallots, ½ cup chopped red onions, ½ cup fresh strawberries, and sliced green jalapeño peppers to taste. Blend until smooth, then pour the mixture into a saucepan and cook over medium heat for about 5–7 minutes to blend the flavors.

Step 8: Cut the buns in half and toast them in the pan. Add Fontina cheese, lettuce, tomato, jalapeños, and the prepared sauce to the sesame buns.

Step 9: Place the patty on the bun, top with caramelized onions, and close with the other half of the bun. Serve with caramelized zucchini on the side and enjoy your burger.

GEEZ SHRIMP & KIMCHI NOODLE SALAD

SERVES: 2 – 4

INGREDIENTS:

- 1 Lb Medium Size Fresh Cleaned Deveined Shrimp
- 1 Pack Of Kimchi Noodles Per Serving
- 1 Tbsp Kimchi Kick Spice
- 1 Tbsp Slap Ya Mama
- 1 Tbsp Shrimp Seasoning

For Iceberg Salad

- Lettuce
- Tomato
- Red Onions
- Sliced Carrots

DIRECTIONS:

Step 1: Rinse the shrimp well under cold water and pat them dry with a paper towel. Place them in a bowl and sprinkle evenly with Kimchi Kick spice, Slap Ya Mama seasoning, and shrimp seasoning. Toss gently so that each shrimp is coated with flavor.

Step 2: Heat a skillet with 1–2 tablespoons of olive oil over medium-high heat. Once hot, arrange the shrimp in a single layer. Cook each side for about 2–3 minutes until the shrimp turn pink and curl slightly. Remove from the pan and set aside.

Step 3: Boil water in a medium pot and cook the Kimchi noodles following the package directions. When tender, drain them and let them cool slightly so they do not stick together. Place them in a large mixing bowl.

Step 4: Wash the lettuce, tomatoes, red onions, and carrots thoroughly. Chop the vegetables into bite-sized pieces.

Step 5: Place a serving of noodles on a plate, top with cooked shrimp, and add the fresh iceberg salad on the side. Drizzle with your favorite salad dressing.

Hot Tip: When frying shrimp, avoid crowding the pan. Cooking them in batches prevents steaming and keeps them crisp and flavorful.

GEEZ GINGER TERIYAKI STOVE TOP CHICKEN

SERVES: 2 – 4

INGREDIENTS:

- 1–2 Leg-Thigh Portions

Geez Ginger Teriyaki Sauce

- 1/2 Cup Whole Ginger, Cut Up
- 1 Bottle Teriyaki Sauce
- 1/2 Cup Frank's Red Wing Sauce
- 1/4 Cup Nonna Pia's Balsamic Sauce
- 1/2 Cup Orange Juice
- 1 Tbsp Ground Ginger
- 1–2 Tbsp Brown Sugar

DIRECTIONS:

Step 1: Wash the leg-thigh portions under cold water and pat dry. Rub the chicken with butter and ground ginger. Place it on a hot grill and cook until both sides are browned.

Step 2: Pour ½ cup of orange juice into the pan or grill-safe skillet with the chicken. Let it reduce slightly to concentrate the flavor.

Step 3: In a saucepan, combine ginger, teriyaki sauce, Frank's Red Wing sauce, balsamic sauce, brown sugar, and remaining orange juice. Simmer for a few minutes until blended and slightly thickened.

Step 4: Pour the ginger teriyaki sauce over the browned chicken, cover, and cook for 10–15 minutes. Reduce the heat to low and continue cooking until the chicken reaches an internal temperature of 160°F.

Step 5: Remove from heat and let it rest briefly before serving. Enjoy with rice, noodles, or salad.

Hot Tip: Tenderize dark meat with a standard tenderizer a few hours before cooking. This makes the chicken softer and allows the sauce to cling beautifully during simmering.

GEEZ SWEET & SOUR CRANBERRY CHUTNEY TURKEY CHOPS

SERVES: 2 – 4
INGREDIENTS:

- 2 Large Turkey Chops

Geez Turkey Chutney Cranberry Sauce (TCCS)

- 1 cup Cranberry Chutney
- 1/2 cup Sweet & Sour Sauce
- 1/2 bottle Teriyaki Sauce
- 1/4 cup Nonna Pia's Balsamic Glaze
- 2 Tbsp Butter
- 1–2 tsp Cornstarch

DIRECTIONS:

Step 1: Rub the turkey chops with smoked salt, black pepper, and butter. Place them on a grill or grill pan and lightly brown them on both sides. Remove and set aside.

Step 2: In another pan, combine the drippings from the grill pan with cranberry chutney, sweet and sour sauce, teriyaki sauce, balsamic glaze, butter, and cornstarch. Simmer until the sauce thickens and the flavors blend.

Step 3: Add the browned turkey chops to the sauce. Simmer together for 5 minutes so the meat absorbs the flavor.

Step 4: Place the turkey chops on a plate and spoon extra sauce over the top. Serve with rice, potatoes, or vegetables.

Enjoy!

GEEZ APPLE TERIYAKI PORK CHOPS

SERVES: 2 – 4

INGREDIENTS:

- 1–2 Green Apples
- 2 -4 Pork Chops
- Smoked Salt
- Butter or Oil

Geez Apple Teriyaki Sauce

- ¼ cup chopped green apples
- ½ sliced long way green apples
- 1/2 bottle Teriyaki sauce
- 1/4 cup Nonna Pia's Balsamic Glaze
- 1 tsp Slap Ya Mama
- 2 Tbsp Butter
- 1–2 tsp Cornstarch

DIRECTIONS:

Step 1: Rinse the pork chops under cold water and pat them dry with paper towels. Lightly tenderize the pork chops with a meat tenderizer and set aside.

Step 2: Heat a grill pan with butter and lightly fry the pork chops on both sides until browned. Remove from the pan.

Step 3: In a separate pan, combine teriyaki sauce, balsamic glaze, Slap Ya Mama seasoning, butter, and cornstarch. Stir and simmer until the sauce thickens and flavors blend.

Step 4: Place the browned pork chops in a baking dish or oven-safe pan. Layer the sliced green apples on top of the chops, then pour some of the apple teriyaki sauce over them.

Step 5: Cover and bake at 350°F (175°C) for 20–25 minutes, or until the pork reaches an internal temperature of 145°F. Baste the apples and chops with extra sauce halfway through for more flavor.

Step 6: Plate the pork chops topped with baked apples and drizzle with more sauce. Serve hot with extra sauce on the side.

Hot Tip: Use smoked salt instead of regular salt on pork chops because it adds a rich, wood-fired flavor that balances the sweetness of the apples and sauce.

Copyright © 2025 by

All Rights Reserved.

No part of this publication can be copied, shared, or stored by electronic, mechanical, or digital means, including photocopying, scanning, recording, or uploading to any system without prior written consent from the copyright holder and publisher.

Garcia Stone

9 798993 525839

www.ingramcontent.com/pod-product-compliance
Lightning Source LLC
Chambersburg PA
CBHW060857090426
42736CB00026B/3499